HOW TO BECOME A PRIVATE INVESTIGATOR

BREAK INTO THE INDUSTRY WITH LITTLE OR NO EXPERIENCE

KURT BREETVELT

The author is based in New Zealand. However, as much as possible, international language and investigative terms have been used.

Links: There are many links to books and articles throughout this book. All the links and references are summarized at the end of the book.

Opening

So, you want to be a private investigator? Great!

You have a desire to enter one of the most exciting professions available. One where no two days are the same. One where you are constantly challenged and need to remain alert and engaged. One where you'll regularly stop and think '...and I'm actually getting paid for this!'

The outlook for private investigators has never been brighter. As the industry has matured, so too have the opportunities. Private investigators are an accepted and necessary part of many legal procedures. Not only that, new technology is opening up ways for private investigators to add value to their clients and expand the areas in which they can assist.

According to the US Bureau of Labor Statistics, the job outlook for private investigators is expected to grow by 8% over the next 10 years.

The opportunity is there. And there are countless books and resources online that show you exactly how to do the work of a private investigator. As someone with no experience, it's never been easier to become self-taught.

You know the work is there. You know you want to do it. If you've read enough or done some training already you might even know how to do the work. But how do you actually get that work in the first place?

What is the first step you need to take right now in order to become a private investigator? Not just getting your license, but getting your first few cases.

That is what this book is for.

There are plenty of other good books out there, especially when it comes to training. However, most of them have been written by seasoned investigators who have been on the job for 30 years and certainly haven't had to apply for a new job in the last couple of decades.

I wanted to write this book now, before I forgot what it was like to be in your shoes.

A few years ago, I was in the position you are now. I had wanted to be a private investigator for years, but I had put it off thinking that I needed a 'normal' job. And besides, how would I become one with no real experience?

Then one day I got made redundant from my 'normal' job. The best break (in disguise) that I ever had. I received a good pay-out, I had a side business that would support me for a few months. I had the motivation, and now I finally had the time.

I was lucky, getting my license was easy. It may not be that easy for you but that's ok, we'll cover that. The real difficulty is getting those first few jobs, that experience that is so highly valued in this industry. That foot in the door.

It took me six months to get my first role in an investigative organization. Six long months! I could have given up; a lot of people have in much a shorter time. Would you?

But during those six months I read over 20 books and countless articles. I started my own business. I did practice investigations. I sent letters, I visited people, I hustled. Most of all, I learnt what it takes to get your foot in the door.

This book is six months of learning. I wish I had something like it when I started.

We cover everything from getting your license, personal attributes, equipment to start with, what to expect, how to get your first role and likely jobs in your first year. On top of that, you'll come away with concrete actionable steps.

Before we start that though, we'll go through a few reasons why you shouldn't be a private investigator. If this is the first book you're reading you may not have had a chance to really think through what being an investigator is like. Perhaps you're still in the research phase or are generally unsure of whether it's really for you. That's fine. Hopefully this section will give you a lot more clarity, and it might be the reality check you need.

Knowing when to stop something is just as important as knowing when to pursue it.

I do hope you enjoy this book and get a lot of value out of it. I've written it specifically for you.

If you have any questions or comments, I'd love to hear from you. You can email me at hello@kurt.nz

Contents

Introduction

The chase

He slowly walks down the gangplank, struggling under the weight of two heavily laden backpacks. That fits the description, but is it the guy I'm after? A quick double check of his picture on my phone confirms it. Back to watching him through my video camera.

A container truck blocks my view. By the time it clears he's disappeared. Damn! Two seconds later he reappears, he's stashed the bags behind the gangplank and is sitting, waiting. This could be a while, you never know how long for.

A taxi pulls up. A struggle to get the bags in the cab and then he's in the back, taxi heading towards the exit, straight past me. Video camera down, engine started ready for a vehicle tail. One car in-between us, perfect. It's a fairly short tail from the port to the train station. The taxi drops him off right next to the platform.

Heart starts beating faster. I need to find a park and get on that platform before the next train. A quick left turn and there's a park. I cut off a white van going for the same spot. A quick check of my equipment, all in the bag. Video camera, phone, hat, water, check. I'm already running towards the platform while I quickly lock the car. Around the corner, sprinting up the stairs and onto the platform. Just before I get to the top I slow to a casual walk. I'm just a guy finishing work, on my way back home. I've already got my headphones in listening to music...in reality I'm on the phone, in contact with my partner who is still in his own vehicle. I'm puffing and my heart's pounding, I fight to stay looking relaxed. Deep breaths.

There's the guy. Sitting on the bench with the two bags. I still don't know where he's heading. A short wait and the train pulls up, it's heading right into town. A quick update to my partner who starts driving, hoping to be able to beat us to town. I then settle in for the ride. I'm behind him, about ten seats back, across the aisle. A good opportunity to get a bit more video on my phone, more evidence for the client.

Half an hour later we're in town. Traffic's been good and my partner has beaten us there. I spot him as we go up the escalator, I'm about ten meters behind the subject. I exchange glances with my partner and he picks up the tail. I can hang back. I take a parallel route to the subject, cautious to not get caught in his path.

It's a slow walk as his backpacks are so heavy. He stops countless times to rest. Eventually we make it to the ferry terminal. How many forms of public transport is this guy going to take? It's a fairly busy terminal. Good. Plenty of opportunity to mingle in the crowd and get a bit closer.

It starts to rain. Everyone cowers under the meagre shelter there. Not our subject. He's walked too far carrying heavy bags to worry about a little bit of rain. The ferry pulls up, people board quickly. The crew help the guy with his heavy bags, after all, he's not that young and it is pouring with rain. Again, I'm settling in for the ride.

As we reach the island everyone has already crowded around the exit, eager to get off. The subject is one of the first in line, there's quite a crowd between us. Be careful not to lose him in the terminal. He won't be walking too fast though.

As we go up the ramp, I see a woman come down the ramp to help him with the bags. Who's she? They place them both on one of the benches and open them up. Really? In this public place? I'm still in the crowd moving towards the exit. A small group breaks away towards the benches. I walk in behind. I have to see what's in the bags and hear what they're saying.

Bingo! It's the goods. And they're being none too shy about discussing exactly what they've got and where they got it. I hear it all, still hidden by the milling crowd.

They close the bags and head towards the exit. I don't have to be too careful about my cover now, we know what they've got. Now to be a bit bolder in getting evidence. I walk slightly ahead and to the side of them. They're still walking slowly, and the crowds are dying down. My cell phone is in my hand by my side, recording video, and I can hear exactly what they're saying. She's putting in an order for the next items he's going to help himself to, from the clients' stock.

They put the bags in a car, hop in and drive off. Too late and too remote to try and get a vehicle to follow them. It doesn't matter, we know where he lives, and I've got the evidence, I've got it all. A visit to him the next day with the evidence is all we need for a full confession, return of stolen goods and voluntary repayments towards his previous offending. Job done, client happy.

How on earth did I go from sitting in an office looking at spreadsheets all day to becoming a private investigator? From office politics to foot and vehicle surveillance. From being stuck in traffic to detecting fraud and getting confessions.

It started as a wild idea. Something I'd love to do but couldn't see how to. For years this idea sat there and ate away at me. I did other things instead, I went to university, got a job in marketing, progressed to management. Did everything that 'normal' people should do. But still I had that idea. But surely, being a private investigator wasn't really a viable career choice? Besides, I had no experience.

It took redundancy from my comfortable job to give me the motivation I needed. And that's when I decided, 'it's now or never'. It wasn't an easy road. It took time, commitment, a lot of waiting and not a small amount of feeling like I'm out of my depth.

I'm here to prove that becoming a private investigator with little or no experience can be done. Not only that, I'm here to show you how.

Section 1: Becoming a private investigator

In this section you will:

- Find out whether this career is really for you by asking some serious questions
- Learn the ideal process to becoming a P.I.
- Find out how to get your license, and options if you can't
- Think about other skills you have that are valuable to companies
- Discover whether courses are valuable or not
- See the common and uncommon backgrounds investigators come from
- Learn the traits common to all good investigators, as well as the skills necessary to do the job
- Start collecting the necessary equipment

Reasons why you shouldn't become a private investigator

Working as a private investigator is an exciting and rewarding prospect. But be under no illusions, there are many difficult aspects of the job. Coupled with the excitement, there can also be a lot of boredom sitting on stakeouts or sifting through documents. You don't necessarily deal with happy people all the time, on the contrary. It can also be a very seasonal job, with irregular hours and income.

Before you even begin the process, you need to decide whether it's really for you. You need to ask yourself a lot of questions. Later in the book I'll go through a 'typical' day which will give you some idea of what to expect.

In the meantime, have a look at these questions and honestly answer with a 'yes' or 'no'.

- You prefer to work normal daytime hours, and you like to be able to go home from work, switch your phone off and not have to think about it until the next day.
- You can't afford to take a pay cut, and you certainly couldn't go for a few months without any income while you get trained.
- You don't like to have uncomfortable conversations with people, and you don't like confrontation.

- You like a steady paycheck; you like to know exactly how much you're going to earn each month.
- You get bored easily and you don't like waiting. You couldn't sit in car for a few hours with potentially nothing happening.
- You don't like writing reports.
- You don't have very good attention to detail.
- You always like to feel safe and comfortable. You don't like any risk.

If you said 'yes' to any of these questions, you need to think seriously about whether this is the right career for you. It's not an automatic disqualification, but if you can't find a way to turn that 'yes' into a 'no', then you're going to have a difficult time of it.

If you honestly said 'no' to most, or all of the questions, then congratulations, you're ready to take the next step.

There are many ways to become a private investigator if you have prior experience. Unfortunately, if you don't have experience, there is really only one way.

You need to gain experience by working for someone else. You cannot gain this experience by doing a course or reading a book. These things may help show you what to do, but eventually you need to actually do the work.

This is the process I followed. In my country of New Zealand, I was able to get my license with almost no experience (I had some prior military experience which helped get the license but was not really helpful for cases).

1. Get your license
2. Start working on your own cases
3. Make yourself a valuable addition to a larger firm
4. Get the experience

If you can't get your license without prior experience, then it changes to this:

1. Make yourself a valuable addition to a larger firm
2. Get the experience
3. Get your license

Get your license

If possible, you want to get your license first. This will vary depending on what state you're in, some require prior experience, some don't. If you can get your license now, that should be your first step.

There are some links to licensing requirement for most countries at the end of this book.

Getting your license says to any potential employer that you're motivated, you're legally allowed to work, you may have had some background checks done on you and you're committed to becoming a private investigator.

An employer will take someone with a license over someone without, any day of the week. It means they don't have to do that for you, and it tends to weed out the dreamers from the doers.

Start working on your own cases

Getting your license is one thing, getting paid work is another. Before approaching potential employers, it's a good idea to start developing your own cases.

If you can go to an employer with a resume showing that you've been active, motivated and already have a few cases under your belt, this will help greatly. My advice is to pick ones with a low risk of failure. I.e. document service, simple surveillance, traces etc. In fact, those were the exact type of cases I started on while looking for a company to work for.

Don't be afraid to say 'no' to a case if you think you don't have enough experience for it.

As you do this, you'll gain an understanding of what it's like to work for clients, run a business, develop cases, report etc. The idea is not to build up a massive portfolio of cases and try and earn a lot of money straight away, as this is almost impossible.

In reality, you'll only get a few cases, and simple ones at that. But this is enough to ensure that when you start working for someone you won't be completely green. You'll know your way around government departments already, you'll know what clients are like and you'll be able to step in with a bit of confidence.

It's all an indicator to a potential employer that you're competent and motivated.

Make yourself a valuable addition to a larger firm

This is by far the most important thing you can do on your road to becoming a private investigator. It's a simple idea. Put yourself in such a position that an employer can't help but think they'd be better off with you. It requires thinking in the opposite way of how we normally think. Instead of thinking 'what can this employer do for me, how can they help me become a P.I.?' you need to think 'how can I help this person, what do they need right now, what skills do I have to make their business better?'

Everything before this step has been working towards this. Getting your license eliminates work your potential employer needs to do and provides them some reassurance. Getting your own cases shows them that you're commercially minded, can deal with people and could increase their business. Now you need to show them how much better their business would be with you.

The first step is to picture what it's like for the manager of a successful investigation firm. I can testify to the fact that they get dozens of phone calls and emails a week from people wanting to work for them. The vast majority are clearly dreamers. They don't have a license, they can't hold down a job and they're very easy to ignore. This is what the manager is expecting when they pick up the phone or open an email. They're ready to say no.

You need to be the minority. A breath of fresh air for the manager. Someone they can start to picture working for them. Someone who can solve a specific set of problems for their business right now. Someone who can add immediate value.

The first step is to identify what other skills you have that can help their business. Sure, you might not have any investigative experience, but everyone has some sort of experience that is valuable to an organization. You need to identify this and match them to what the company needs.

When I first started calling companies, I tried to display my skills as a P.I. I had done some of my own cases, I could do simple surveillance, I had an inquisitive mind, my report writing was outstanding, and I could conduct interviews. These are all good things, but most potential candidates are going to have these exact skills as well.

Over the next few months, I slowly changed my tactics a bit. Instead of focusing on investigative skills, I started looking at other skills I have. I actually have a business degree, so surely I could help businesses on their marketing and management side. I was a lot younger than most investigators coming out of the police force, so I had various social media experience that they didn't have. In the end, I came up with a list like this:

- General marketing experience

- Can build/develop websites
- Management and systems experience
- A digital native (brought up in the age of computers)
- Meticulous report writing
- Excellent working knowledge of all forms of social media
- IT experience (including cloud computing)
- Ability to blend in with and relate to a younger crowd
- Enthusiasm for jobs older investigators would consider boring
- An image that doesn't shout 'cop' whenever I walk into a situation

Suddenly people started paying a bit more attention. I started getting replies to emails and calls, and I started getting meetings with people.

Eventually I got a job with the one firm I had really wanted to work for. After they hired me, they told me that it wasn't for my investigative skills as I was still very green. It was because they wanted someone to develop their website, work on a social media marketing strategy and help them with their IT needs. Nothing to do with investigation!

As much as it hurt my ego (not really, I knew my limitations), they didn't hire me for my investigative experience, it was because of my persistence and the marketing help I could bring.

I worked on all those things for them, and at every opportunity I worked on their cases as well. The other skills I had were a foot in the door. Once they saw that I was actually valuable as an investigator as well they never looked back! I was the triple threat. I applied myself to investigation, I was enthusiastic and motivated, and I had other business skills that helped them.

Don't automatically think that you're at a disadvantage because you weren't a police officer or similar. There are some potential downsides to employing ex-law enforcement. Often, they need a consistent pay check as that's what they're used to. They don't like the boring jobs as they've done enough of them already and they aren't as keen to pursue new cases as they're used to getting cases handed to them.

I've seen many investigators quit the police force, become a P.I. and then very quickly move on to something else for these reasons.

Many also find the transition difficult. They're used to having some sort of authority and power. And usually a uniform that demands a certain amount of respect. When they become an ordinary citizen doing investigative work, they often find that their official form of questioning or enquiries doesn't get them very far.

Of course, this isn't true for all of them, but it helps to know how you can differentiate yourself from them and give employers something new to look for.

Ideally, you'll want to work for a medium-sized investigative or legal firm handling commercial cases. This will ensure a variety of work and the opportunity for a good relationship with your manager. There are also a handful of major companies that handle insurance claims surveillance. These tend to be a little harder to deal with, the hourly rate is lower and there's not a consistent workflow. However, they can be a good option for a year or so to get some surveillance experience.

Get the experience

Once you're actually working for someone, getting the experience is the easy part. It just comes with time. The more cases you can be involved in, the more you put your hand up and say 'yes' to things, the quicker you'll get this experience.

In New Zealand, most investigators are contractors. They have their own business, but they mainly receive work by contracting to larger investigative firms. This is great for flexibility, but often it can feel like you're juggling many jobs, cases and employers at once.

When I decided I needed experience, and finally got a contract with the investigative firm I wanted, I stuck with them. I didn't go to any other firms hoping to get more work, I concentrated on being the best contractor I could be for the one firm.

This did two things. It showed loyalty to the company that gave me my first break and in turn it made sure I was given plenty of work from them. Yes, it did mean that if work for them was quiet, it would be quiet for me too, but when work was busy, I was their contractor of choice.

I made a point of going into the office everyday even if there was no work on (most contractors would stay at home or try to find something else to do, waiting for a call). Because I was working on their marketing as well, I still had something to do. Usually around 10am the lead investigator would get a call, a new case, or there would be a development in a current case. He'd need someone to go and do some surveillance. Normally this would lead to him calling his contractors seeing who was available. But because I was right there across the room it would be given to me. Not because I was any better than his other contractors, but because I was available right now and could be briefed straight away.

The next day he'd need someone to help on an urgent interview, or he'd need some documents served on someone, or he needed some surveillance reviewed, or he was under the gun trying to get a report out and needed someone to check it…. etc.

This happened day after day. Eventually, I did become better than the other contractors because I was being given more work than any of them. Simply because I was committed and available, I was the contractor of choice. Not only did I get more work, I got a huge variety of work. The more I proved myself in little things, the more complex my tasks would get.

There were some tasks that I didn't get paid for, i.e. I'd be going with an experienced investigator on an interview, purely for the sake of learning. This was fine with me. In the main I did get paid, and any cases I didn't get paid for I put down to experience and learning. You don't get paid when you're going to college, so this was no different.

An investigative firm is the same as any other firm. When something needs doing, they'll generally pick the closest person to hand (especially when things are busy). Not only that, they'll pick the person who is the most enthusiastic (and therefore wants to do a good job). It's human nature, if someone is working for you with a cheerful attitude, you'll want to keep feeding them work.

So, if you want to get as much experience as possible, do this:

- Be immediately available, convenience trumps experience
- Be enthusiastic and cheerful
- Put your hand up for everything
- Approach even the most basic task with gusto, it'll lead to greater things

- Be eager to learn, do your own study and ask questions
- Use your initiative, what else could you do that they haven't asked you to do yet?

This is the process I followed. It took me six months to figure it out, but I got there.

If you can, get your license now. Start thinking about how you can add value to an organization now. Start talking to people now.

Whatever you do, start now!

I can't guarantee that things will come quickly, but I can guarantee that if you follow these steps, you'll be in a much better position than almost every other candidate out there.

Legal requirements, getting your license, courses

Getting your license is one of the first steps to take, if you can. There are some countries or states that require a license and some that don't.

On top of that, some require several other things in order to carry out business as a private investigator.

- Individual license
- Agency license
- Examination
- Background/police check
- Proof of training
- Bond
- Insurance
- Firearms permit

There are some links to licensing requirement for most countries at the end of this book.

Always check with your individual licensing authority for up to date licensing requirements and reciprocity agreements (working across state borders).

The requirements for getting a license vary from country to country and state to state. They can range for a simple 'tick the box and pay the fee' process to a system requiring a year or more of investigative experience as well as a police background check and even a bond payment.

What if you can't ever get your license?

There are a few reasons why you wouldn't ever be able to get your license. They vary from country or state, but common ones are:

- Criminal conviction
- Dishonorable discharge from the military
- Unable to satisfy background check requirements

If you're in this category, you have a couple of options. You can either move somewhere that would allow you to get your license. Or, you can work in an area as close to private investigation as possible, that doesn't require a license.

Some examples may be:

- Process serving
- Retrieving public records
- Specialized research
- Registered agent
- Surveillance equipment installation
- Bounty hunting
- Investigative journalism

Most authorities don't require a license for these, check with your licensing authority first.

Remember, if you just want to work on your own investigation (not for a paying client) then you don't need a license. Anyone is allowed to do any legal investigative work for themselves.

As a side note, a very common question I get is: 'do you have any extra rights or authority over an ordinary citizen?'

The answer is no. We do not have any special privileges. We are not police officers (and making someone think that you are is a serious crime), we do not have powers of arrest, we are no different from any ordinary citizen.

The only difference is our attitude and our relationships. And the fact that we have a license, which legally allows us to perform investigations for commercial gain. Because it's our job, of course we know a lot more than an ordinary person about surveillance, online searches, the legal system etc. We use this to our full advantage in the job. We're also curious, tenacious and have great attention to detail.

So, in short, any of our clients have the right to do exactly what we're getting paid to do for them (conducting an investigation). But not everyone has the ability, patience, experience or time to do it. Hence why we're in business.

We are ordinary citizens acting on the instructions of the client, as an agent for them.

Courses

There are dozens of courses available ranging from completely online or by correspondence, to ones run by fairly well-known institutions.

Personally, I never did any of these courses. The reasons for that were twofold.

Firstly, I did a lot of my own research on how to become a P.I. and how to get experience and I did not see any of these courses offering anything more valuable than what I could find out for myself. I wanted to become a P.I., I should be able to conduct some pretty good research myself! These courses tended to die out as quickly as they started up. The main reason was that they couldn't get placements for their graduates and so they lost relevance.

Secondly, and more importantly, every single experienced private investigator I spoke to or read articles on said the same thing. They did not regard these courses as relevant or helpful. In fact, it seemed that if you took these courses you automatically got labelled a 'dreamer' or 'wannabe', so they may have even been more detrimental than helpful.

So regardless of whether the course has some value or not, if the person you're wanting to work for doesn't value it then it's not relevant to getting a job as a P.I. There are plenty of other ways to get experience. Sure, they may contain some good tips and information presented in a structured way, but it's nothing you can't find out yourself without having to pay the fees.

If you do a course, or have done one already, that's fine, just be careful who you tell!

If you need to do work for any government department (on behalf of the company you work for) often you'll be vetted and have to send in a resume. They generally do not view these courses as relevant experience.

There are papers or degrees you can do through reputable universities or colleges. These would generally be found in their law departments. They can be helpful for very specific areas of investigation, and they may give you credit towards getting your license, depending on where you are.

Common and uncommon backgrounds

After a while in the industry you get to know where investigators tend to come from. In the case of former police officers, often just by looking at them! But regularly you'll come across that person who came from a completely different field, one that you wouldn't expect would lead to a career in private investigation.

There are common backgrounds for most private investigators, but just because you don't have this background doesn't mean you won't make a great investigator. In the next chapter, we'll go over attributes common to investigators (regardless of what background you came from). In the meantime, here are some common and uncommon backgrounds.

Common
- Police officer or other law enforcement role
- Insurance claims adjuster
- Military police or intelligence
- Parent was a P.I.
- Completed a bachelor's degree in criminal justice or similar
- Private internship or online training
- Legal profession

Not so common
- Journalism
- Accounting or finance
- IT specialist
- Security industry
- Other completely non-related industries!

There is a helpful article at pinow.com showing common backgrounds and who private investigators regularly work with.
https://www.pinow.com/resources/how-to-become-a-private-investigator

A number of people have asked me how to get a job as a security contractor or close protection officer. While I have never done these specific roles, I have worked with many people who have. I was offered a role in Papua New Guinea and on ships doing counter-piracy, but it's not what I wanted to do.

From what I've seen, getting a role like this is all about who you know. The people who are hiring just look around among their network. They'd much rather work with people they know and trust. I.e. people they have served with in the military or police force.

Added to that, being a close protection officer (bodyguard) is a very specific role that requires a lot of training. Because you're responsible for someone's life, it's only right that they want the best! So if you are interested in either of these roles, the best way is through the police or military first. You'll make some contacts, build trust and get training.

The amount of people I've suggested this to, who are too impatient to do it, is astounding. They just want to get out there and do the job. Unfortunately it doesn't work that way for these particular roles. And what is a few years in the scheme of things if it leads to something you really want to do? Many people do a college degree for four to five years and still don't know what they want to do!

Back to being a private investigator. As a side note, being a female is not a disadvantage. In fact, in a lot of situations it can be an advantage. In some cases, a client will want a female investigator, especially in domestic cases. This is because, generally speaking, females tend to show more empathy and understanding. They can also be better listeners and appear less threatening.

Females don't usually intimidate an interviewee as much, so can often get more information than a male investigator might.

In the case of allegations (of inappropriate or suggestive behavior during an interview for example), having a female witness present first can often avoid that. One of the oldest tricks in the book for an alleged insurance fraudster who is female, is to accuse the male investigator of sexual harassment. Suddenly the case doesn't become about her alleged fraud, it becomes about you trying to defend your reputation! If you had a female investigator as a witness there in the first place that never would have happened.

We made it standard practice to have a female present whenever conducting an interview with a female.

On the other side of it though, this is an industry that tends to be dominated by men (depending on where you are of course). And there can be some situations that a female by herself can suddenly feel very vulnerable and unsafe in. But as long as you're aware of that first and have a plan to manage this, then a female has as much chance to make it as a male does.

Hopefully this chapter has shown you that you can come from just about any background and be a successful P.I. Additionally, here are some links to how other people got into the industry:

A classroom teacher discovers her love of criminal justice and finds her perfect job.
http://pursuitmag.com/how-became-private-investigator/

A Florida private investigator explains how she learned the tricks of her trade: by catching shoplifters
http://pursuitmag.com/private-investigator-start-loss-prevention/

10 skills journalism brings to private investigations work
http://pursuitmag.com/10-skills-journalism-private-investigations-work/

Q&A: Mike Spencer, Bay Area private investigator
http://pursuitmag.com/mike-spencer-bay-area-private-investigator/

Career spotlight: what I do as a private investigator
https://www.lifehacker.com.au/2016/04/career-spotlight-what-i-do-as-a-private-investigator/

Personal attributes

As we learned in the previous chapter, you may not come from a background that immediately lends itself to private investigation. However, this should not stop you. Provided you have, or can develop or learn, some key qualities.

There are some very specific traits common to almost all private investigators (successful ones at least).

1. Having a thick skin. This is not an easy job and you are not dealing with nice people all the time. You will face abuse and you may be treated like the villain by whomever you're investigating. You need to be able to handle this. Yes, you should try to treat everyone fairly, but you will at times have very uncomfortable conversations. As long as you're staying true to your own values and maintain your integrity, you don't need to worry too much about what people think or say about you.

2. Good verbal and written communication skills. A lot hinges on what you say, both on investigations and in court. You need to be able to communicate, persuade and influence effectively and succinctly. Equally, you need to be able to do the same on paper. Your spelling, grammar and vocabulary need to be excellent. If they're not, at least find someone else who can check or create your reports and correspondence for you. Written communication also includes your ability to keep good records and a tidy system for billing, reporting, compliance etc.

3. Common sense and a logical mind. It's important to remain objective during a case and not be side-tracked or miss the glaringly obvious. You need to be comfortable in all sorts of situations and you need to maintain a clear head during times of stress. You also need to be able to adapt quickly to changing situations, so a good broad knowledge of a lot of areas is useful. Having common sense also means you keep the bigger picture in mind, especially when it comes to your own safety. There is no room for a 'macho' attitude. In dangerous situations, just walk (or run) away.

4. Inquisitiveness and persistence. At the start of a case it's very easy to be overwhelmed with the amount of information and ways you could

begin. You need to be able to start unravelling, and then once you start you need to be able to follow through to its completion.

5. Patience and the ability to work alone. There are no questions about it, you will spend a lot of time waiting. When I say a lot, I mean hours at a time. Whether in a vehicle, in a café or in a holding area. Or you may be working on a lead for days with no real visible progress. And a lot of this may be on your own. You need to be comfortable with this without going out of your mind.

6. Street-smarts or worldly wisdom. You can't be naïve. You will hear all sorts of stories, and everyone is innocent when you first start interviewing them. You need to be able to trust the evidence and your instincts and not believe everything you hear (in fact, you almost need to disbelieve everything until it's verified to be true).

7. A non-judgmental attitude. You generally won't know the full circumstances of the situation so it's not up to you to judge people, nor to take their side. Just concentrate on doing your job as professionally as you can. Having no emotional attachment makes things a lot easier. We're not here to solve crimes or make the world right, we're here to act on instructions from our client. Another reason is, you never know who you will see again or whether you'll eventually need something from them! Treat people with respect and don't burn your bridges.

8. Confidence. The ability to be comfortable in any situation, regardless of how out of place you feel. Yes, some of this needs to be fake confidence because in a lot of cases you will be acting when trying to blend in. You also need to be able to talk to anyone of any background, building a rapport and getting people to open up to you.

9. Professionalism and willingness. Nail these two and you'll have a steady supply of clients. Remember, when they come to you, they're expecting some sort of reassurance. Whether that's a case solved, or if not at least the knowledge that they tried their best and hired a professional. And if you're not only professional, but willing and eager to take on a case (provided that it's a case you would accept) then that's the x factor. Who would you rather work with, a professional who looks bored or one who is enthusiastic?

Skills needed

On top of the traits in the previous chapter, to work as a private investigator you need to have investigative skills, obviously. However, when you're trying to become a private investigator with little or no experience, you're not necessarily going to have these skills.

This is where your personal attributes come in. Whilst the skills can be learned, the attributes I've mentioned in the previous section are absolutely necessary to show that you can in fact learn the skills.

If you want to work for someone else first, having the following hard skills (skills that can be easily learned) before you apply will make you a much better candidate. I would suggest making introductions and applying for roles as you develop these skills. Some will take time and you can't wait until you're an expert before you start working! At least you've made a start and can demonstrate your progress (and initiative) to any potential employer.

- Experience in digital photography, still and video
- Excellent written and verbal communication
- Outstanding report writing
- Knowledge of advanced internet searches
- Experience in all major social media platforms
- Working knowledge of your country/state laws (especially privacy)
- Knowledge of where and how to find court records, and how the court system works
- Basic legal vocabulary
- Good observation and memory

If you start getting your own cases, without working for someone else, then you will also need investigative knowledge to do a good job. On top of that, you will need business and marketing know-how. Being able to work as a private investigator is one thing, being able to bring work into your business is another. The technical knowledge and business knowledge go hand in hand to create a successful business.

If you don't have any of these skills, don't be overwhelmed! This chapter is intended to be an overview. There are plenty of resources at the back of the book where you can go and learn from.

Here is a list of essential equipment. These are the items I use on a regular basis. I haven't gone into too much detail as there are plenty of other articles that do so, and that's more on the training side. But this should give you a good idea of what you'll most likely use in your first year.

Be aware that if a company hires you as a contractor, they will most likely expect you to have your own equipment. Not many firms supply equipment to their contractors these days.

Necessary

- Digital video camera. This must have a number of features such as ability to record in low/no light, a decent optical zoom, compact enough to conceal easily, ability to have a date/time stamp on the recording, tripod mounting point, ideally a viewfinder (not just a fold out screen), SD card recording (for evidence chain of custody).
- Digital camera. Same as above but for taking high quality still shots. Some video cameras have this ability too.
- A burner phone. One you can call and text people on and not have them trace it back to you. Because of the people you'll be dealing with you do need to take your security seriously. Change this phone every few months. You can easily hide your number on calls, so you can theoretically use your normal phone for that, but there's no easy way to hide your number when texting.
- A suitable vehicle. One that can blend in, so pick a common vehicle for the area you're operating in. Make sure it doesn't have any distinguishing or unusual features that will help people remember it. The windows need to be legally tinted so no one can see inside. If possible, ensure the number plate is hidden on your state's motor vehicle database (so it can't be traced to you).
- A smart phone. With GPS, decent camera, voice recording etc. Make sure you have a Bluetooth earpiece so you can be handsfree even if you get out of your vehicle. Battery life is key, I also carry a power pack when I can.
- A Dictaphone/audio recorder. These days you can usually use your phone but the last thing you want to do is run out of battery during an interview. Keeping a separate audio recorder is good insurance.

- Laptop. You'll be doing a lot of work on the road, especially writing reports and transferring photos and video. A tablet will not suffice, you need something that has a good processor and USB ports. I use a Microsoft Surface Pro as it's almost as light as a tablet yet still has complete functionality.

Nice to have

- A covert camera. In most cases I've recorded photo and video on my phone, it does not look suspicious if done correctly as everyone has a phone, and it records the date/time/GPS location in the meta data. However, in some situations a covert camera disguised as a pen, for example, may be necessary. Get the highest resolution one you can and make sure it records date/time.
- A static camera. One that allows you to leave it outside in all weather. It needs to be weatherproof. These often operate on motion detection.

You'll notice that I've left off any mention of firearms or defensive weapons. In New Zealand, even our police force doesn't regularly carry firearms so there's no way an ordinary citizen is allowed to walk around with one. It's similar in a lot of other countries too.

However, of the private investigators in the US that I've spoken to or read, 90% say that they don't recommend carrying one either. If you don't carry one, you're forced to rely on your communication skills and non-confrontational approach when working on a case. This tends to get better results anyway than if you appear threatening in any way. Insurance is also more complicated if you do carry one.

Section review (the essentials)

Do you have what it takes to become a private investigator? In this section, you've seen some reasons why you might not be suited. Do you prefer to work regular, fixed hours? Do you get bored easily? Do you need well-paying work right now? Then perhaps this isn't for you.

If it is, there's an ideal process to follow. Getting your license, working on some of your own cases and getting experience with a larger investigative firm (by making yourself a valuable addition to them). We briefly covered the legal aspects of getting your license, with plenty of helpful links at the back of the book.

If you're thinking about doing a course (online or offline) have a good think about whether it's necessary or not. Talk to prospective employers and get their view on it.

Some common backgrounds of private investigators: police or law enforcement, military, legal profession and insurance. If you don't come from one of these, don't fret! There are plenty of other people who haven't either. As long as you have some key personal attributes such as patience, persistence and inquisitiveness then the investigative skills can be learned.

Action plan

☐   Answer the questions in the first chapter with an honest 'yes' or a 'no'. If any were a 'yes', think hard about whether this is the right career for you.

☐   Start thinking about setting yourself up in business (more on this later). What structure of business? What name?

☐   Start researching investigative companies in your area that you'd like to work for. Which ones look like they're growing? Which ones' work in an area you have an interest in?

☐   Make a list of skills you have right now that could help those companies. Think from their perspective. Could you help them develop a website? Do you have marketing experience? Do you have specific expertise in an area they specialize in?

☐ Find out whether you're eligible to get your license now. If you are, apply for it. There are links to licensing requirements for most countries at the back of this book.

☐ Looking at the personal attributes and skills needed to be a P.I., what areas do you need to work on? Make a list and start doing some research on how you can develop in these areas. Make a start now.

☐ Check your equipment against the equipment list. If you don't have everything, keep an eye out on eBay or similar (second hand is always cheaper).

Section 2: What to expect

In this section you will:

- Review a typical day in the life of a private investigator, including typical (or not so typical) clients and cases
- Get an idea of what salary to expect
- Discover how your personal life will be impacted, and what needs to be managed

A day in the life of a private investigator

I'm not sure what your perception of private investigators is. You may have already done plenty of research and have a fair idea of what they do. Then again, this may be the first thing you read, and the only examples of a P.I. that you have are from movies or TV shows. As with most things on TV (including 'reality' TV), real life is different.

Hopefully reading through this book, and looking at the below example schedule, will dispel any myths and perhaps show you another side that you didn't think about.

Just remember though, if you tell people you're a P.I., the first thing they will think of is whatever TV show they've seen. Often the first question I get is 'do you drive a Ferrari?' This can get annoying if you let it. Just realize that most people are going to be fascinated with the fact that you follow people for a living. And they are genuinely interested in what you do regardless of what their perception is, based on TV shows. Pick your audience though. If you really don't want to talk about it just say you work in accounts (as you will definitely be looking through accounts at some stage as a P.I.).

The first thing to keep in mind is that in most countries, a private investigator does not have any more rights than a private citizen. We're not allowed to drive any faster, we can't arrest people, we can't violate people's reasonable expectation of privacy and we can't go around shooting at people.

Generally, we want to blend in and gather evidence in the most discreet manner possible. This means driving the most common and unremarkable car you can find, wearing clothes that blend in rather than stand out and behaving in such a manner that no one would pay us a second glance.

Yes, there are times when it can be very exciting. But for the most part, we want to be so prepared that not many things are a surprise to us. A slow methodical approach will beat a 'wing-it' attitude almost every time.

Of course, no day is typical, and many times things come up that you need to attend to straight away. However, there are a lot of things that you will do very regularly. As a private investigator, a typical day for me would look something like this:

8am. I'm a little tired this morning as I was out from 7pm to 1am last night on surveillance. The case was a worker's insurance claim. It's a back injury and the claimant states that he can't articulate his back at all. No bending over, no twisting etc. For most of the night he wasn't doing this, but at around midnight he went to a pool hall. It took me a while to get into position, but I finally got some video of him playing a full game including bending over, twisting at various angles and holding the cue behind his back. I've just phoned the client to give them an update and am now compiling the video and photos I took. I'm backing them up and putting them into the case file on my computer. I won't do a report yet as the client wants me to do the same another night.

9am. I've already taken a call from someone wanting me to find out if the government is spying on him. I politely declined. Yes, you do get some interesting people calling you.

10.30am. I have a meeting with another client who suspects that his accounts payable person is somehow siphoning money into his own account. He has some valid suspicions but not enough technical knowledge to really look into his accounts system to get to the bottom of it. I'm drafting a proposal letter to him now covering our fees and what steps we would take. Could be a good case for us.

12pm. I've had a few emails confirming my appearance in court next week, from the police prosecutor. I'm presenting my evidence as a witness on a case I worked on last year. It takes so long for these things to go through court. I grab a bite to eat from the café down the road. I try not to eat at my desk as that's a very bad habit.

1pm. There's a new case I'm working on, similar to the accounts payable case. This time it's the dispatch manager. She's allegedly writing off stock as damaged and then selling it through her cousin's company online. I've been doing some web, social media and database searches to see exactly what she owns. I'm trying to see whether she's living within the means of someone on her salary or appears to spend more than she legally earns. I'm also preparing a surveillance plan for tomorrow night. She's working late, with little supervision. Will be a good chance to observe any stock movements. If that doesn't work, we'll look at installing a hidden camera in the warehouse area. The client hasn't approved costs for that yet.

I also have another trademark case. Someone is wanting to register a trademark however there is another company with the brand name listed on their website. I need to find out whether they're actively selling the product under that brand name or whether it's dormant (not actively used) and therefore available to trademark by the other company. I'll do an extensive web search and the visit the store later this afternoon to make some enquiries.

1.30pm. In the early afternoon, I get a call from a client, she's had some information that her ex-husband, who is supposed to be looking after the children today, is drinking with his mates and leaving them unsupervised. It's a custodial case and this could be exactly what she needs. I drop everything and quickly drive out to her ex-husbands house. I already have everything I need in my car and it's full of fuel. I fill it up each morning on the way to work as you never know what's going to happen that day.

The husband doesn't appear to be home. About 10 minutes later he walks up the road with the children. It looks like they've been to the park. They go inside and start preparing afternoon tea. No evidence of drinking and certainly none of his mates about. This is the third time that's happened. The client may be grasping at straws, but I will follow her instructions as long as I'm getting paid. I drive back to the office, I phone the client with an update on the way. I'll only report the facts though. Some clients want you to see things that aren't really there, to support their case!

3.30pm. I'm back at the office, I tidy a few emails up and decide to call it a day. I've had a long night, and you never know. I may get a call later tonight with something urgent. In the meantime, I'll go home to spend some time with my wife and kids.

As you can see, the day wasn't all car chases and interviewing people. A lot of it was paperwork, planning and talking to clients!

Just remember, almost everything you do will be the result of prior planning. Then once it's done it will require some type of report.

Clients will be pushy and want results now, but make sure you stick to a logical process and aren't running around putting out fires.

I put 'typical' in inverted commas as there is probably no such thing. As a private investigator, you will meet all sorts of weird and wonderful people. Whilst their behavior and appearance may not be quite what you're used to, their reasons for coming to a private investigator can be separated into two categories: personal/domestic cases, and commercial cases.

Domestic cases can include:

- Catching a cheating spouse
- Infidelity and divorce cases
- Surveillance or following someone
- Locating birth parents or adopted children
- Gathering evidence for a child custody case
- Locating or tracing someone
- Personal injury cases

Domestic cases are the ones that can turn messy very quickly. The company I worked for stayed away from these ones as much as possible. My boss gave a perfect example why. Say a woman comes to you convinced that her husband is cheating on her. You conduct the investigation and find no evidence to support this. You report back to her and she insists that you're wrong and refuses to pay. On the other hand, you may find out he is cheating. You report back to her, she's heartbroken, her life falls apart and she doesn't pay anyway. Either way it's bad. There are not many domestic cases that have a happy ending.

One that did still stands out in my mind. I had a client approach me wanting to track down a woman he had been with for a year. Out of the blue she had told him that she had been cheating on him, was pregnant with someone else's baby and was moving to another part of the country. She then left abruptly.

He took a while to process this and then started working out some dates. He thought that the baby might in fact be his. If it was, he wanted to make sure it was at least being looked after and was not in a bad domestic situation. He decided to investigate and see if we could find out whether the baby was his. To make matters more complicated, he was still married to a different woman! He had split with her for a year (the year he was with the other woman), and then got back together again. So, everything had to be done quietly.

As far as he was concerned, he just wanted to do right by the baby. When clients come to you with cases like this, you tend to be very wary about what they say to you. Did he want to do right by the baby? Or did he just want to make sure his wife didn't find out about his fling and potential baby? Either way, you have to learn to do what you're paid for and not make judgements, as long as taking the case isn't compromising your own integrity. Don't ever be afraid to say 'no' to a case. No case is worth more than your integrity and reputation, or doing something illegal.

Anyway, after a lot of social media investigation (social media has helped investigators considerably in the last 10 or so years), I managed to track her down. After some surveillance, I obtained photos of her, the baby and the unknown male she was living with. One look at the baby and the male she was with and we didn't need to go any further. I've never seen a baby look so much like their father! This included a completely different skin color to my client. No need for a paternity test there.

My client was happy, the baby wasn't his, he was back with his wife and there were no further issues. This was a rare exception though.

As a rule, for any domestic cases we did take on, we insisted on payment or a retainer up front (up to what we thought it would cost to do the investigation).

Commercial cases can include:

- Investigating fraud or shrinkage (under-performing departments) in an organization
- Surveillance
- Background or pre-employment checks
- Serving trespass notices on behalf of a property owner
- Process serving, document service, court summons, subpoenas etc.
- Investigating workers claim compensation
- Accident and insurance claim investigations
- Locating or tracing someone, missing persons, skip tracing, finding deadbeat parents
- Credit reports
- Repossessions and debt collection
- Investigations, on instructions from the defense in a trial
- Cyber-crime or counter-surveillance
- Bounty hunting

- Security audits

Commercial cases were the bread and butter for my company. A typical case would be a medium sized business with either a branch or a department that wasn't performing as well as they used to, with no logical reason.

We'd conduct some surveillance, investigation, interviewing and a review of all systems and accounts. From that we'd find out that one of their accounts payable staff had been creating false invoices under their own bank account, or their dispatch manager had been diverting some stock to sell on the side. The pattern was typical and the resolution tended to be a lot cleaner than a domestic case.

With the way technology is changing the world, there are more opportunities for private investigators opening up. With a bit of creativity, there are many more uncommon cases such as:

- Investigating school zone fraudsters
- Advising parents on their child's technology/social media use
- In-depth competitor analysis and research
- Background checks on potential romantic partners
- Doing an in-depth check on the client and advising them if there's anything that could be used to blackmail them
- Penetration testing for a premises, website or database
- Research/investigation/background checks for charities or not-for-profits

There may not be such a thing as a 'typical' client, but there is a logical process that can be applied to every case, regardless of how strange it may seem.

As far as actual volume of work goes, here is a good article on pinow.com showing the 10 most common specialties of private investigators according to a survey.
https://www.pinow.com/articles/1737/the-10-most-common-specialties-of-private-investigators

They are (in order of frequency):

1. Background checks
2. Civil investigations

3. Surveillance
4. Other (criminal defense, child custody, automobile theft etc.)
5. Insurance investigations
6. Fraud
7. Corporate investigations
8. Accident reconstruction
9. Domestic investigations
10. Infidelity and cheating spouse

The good news for the P.I. industry is that there is more and more work coming our way. The industry has undergone a few changes in the last couple of decades, including the perception in the public's mind.

We're no longer necessarily seen as people who sneak around spying on cheating spouses, we're becoming almost an extension of the legal system. Lawyers use us, government departments use us, law enforcement use us. There are constantly new areas and industries opening up where a P.I. can be useful. Whether out of necessity or whether they genuinely see the value in using a private investigator, the future is looking bright.

Remember, private investigators are in the information business. Not just the surveillance business, or insurance, or background checks. But we're in the business of providing information. With that in mind, how many different areas do you think that can be applied to now?

Salary

One of the big questions when starting out. "How much do I get paid?"

This varies depending on the case, type of client, and your experience.

As a beginner or employee in the US you might be doing work for $13 to $40 an hour (likely at the lower end). Once you gain more experience and have your own business this can be upwards of $150 an hour.

Not only does the hourly rate vary, the amount of cases coming in can be even more up and down. It tends to be either feast or famine. A lot of investigators I know have another job or side hustle going on. Something they can focus on when cases dry up, yet something they can almost ignore when they start flowing in again.

Before you get into this industry you must accept that fact that there is no guaranteed paycheck each month. Not only that, you may go for months without getting paid when you first start out.

When I first got my license, it took me a full six months before I got my first paying role working for someone else. I had done a few of my own jobs, but there's only very few things you can do with no experience and I knew I needed to partner with a larger firm to be able to get that experience. Luckily, I had another business that was able to support me during this time, and I had a bit of money saved up.

We tend to make rash decision when under financial pressure. If you want to be a private investigator, best to take that pressure off. Settle in for the long haul when going for your first role. Make sure you have enough funding to cover up to a year without a salary, and ideally another couple of years on perhaps a lower salary than what you came from.

Here are the salary ranges by country for a beginner to intermediate investigator working for someone else (i.e. not running their own business).

United States
- $13-$43 an hour
- Median rate is $24
- Median salary is $50,090

Canada
- $14-$39 an hour
- Median rate is $23
- Median salary is $46,480
  https://neuvoo.ca/salary/?job=Private%20Investigator

UK
- £8-£41 an hour
- Median rate is £23
- Median salary is £46,480
  https://www.indeed.co.uk/salaries/private-investigator-Salaries,-England

Australia
- $26-$50 an hour
- Median rate is $39
- Median salary is $78,000
  https://www.payscale.com/research/AU/Job=Private_Detective_or_Investigator/Salary

New Zealand
- $28-$60 an hour
- Average rate is $45
- Average salary is $75,000
  https://www.glassdoor.co.nz/Salaries/investigator-salary-SRCH_KO0,12.htm

The private investigations industry is definitely one that can have an effect on your personal life. There are certain considerations, and things you will need to manage, if you decide to go down this path.

I've covered a lot of safety considerations throughout the book, so I won't go over that again. What I will go into is the changes you may find in your personal life if you become a P.I.

The obvious one is working hours. This is not a 9-5 job, nor is it shift work with set hours. You will do the hours that the case requires, and often they are not the most sociable hours. 5-11pm tends to be a very common period of surveillance. You don't do this every day, but I was doing this at least twice a week when I started out.

The good news is there are two areas to your work. One is the investigation, which tends to be inflexible i.e. you don't have a lot of control over what time of day that happens. Things unfold, you realize you need to do surveillance right away, or interview someone urgently. You need to be prepared to do what it takes to solve the case.

The second is the administration, which is report writing, billing/invoicing, filing etc. Anything that supports the business. This is usually pretty flexible. So, if you do stay up late on surveillance you can usually start later the next day (unless you have something pressing to do).

So be aware of that. If you like to be at home at 6pm every night having dinner with the family then there will be a conflict. That being said, you won't (or shouldn't) be expected to work huge hours every week. This is not sustainable no matter what stage of life you're at. The hours that you do work will just be at various times of the day.

Another thing to consider is the fact that you will have the most interesting job compared to almost everyone you meet. Be careful who you tell, because it has consequences.

This is mainly because you don't want to be compromised while on a case. The last thing you want to happen when you're following someone is to be confronted by someone you recently met with 'hey, you're that P.I., are you spying on someone right now?'

Or worse, you may be investigating that very person you met at the party last week.

I live in a large city (over 1.3 million people) so the chances of me running into someone who I may investigate, or would blow my cover, is fairly slim. If you live in a small town, you'll need to be more careful.

The second reason to be careful is because of the amount of attention it does get. Most people haven't met a private investigator so of course they're going to be interested in what you do. You will get the same questions over and over again. Most of the time that's fine, but if you want to have a relaxing night then come up with a cover story. I usually told people what my other business was (a lot of private investigators have other things they're involved in to support them in the quiet times).

If you do tell people, expect these common responses:

- Do you drive a Ferrari?
- You don't look like a P.I. (this is a good thing)
- I'd better be careful what I say, you might investigate me
- So, do you sneak around catching cheating husbands or wives?
- How did you get into that?
- What's your most interesting case?

I tended to tell people about 50% of the time what I did for a job. When I did, I knew exactly what was coming and I had my answers prepared.

The last thing I'll cover here is one that anybody working in the law enforcement/military/public safety sphere knows about all too well.

If you're not careful, you can become callous and have trouble trusting the general public. You get to see the worst side of people most days and it's easy to start thinking that everybody is like this. Untrustworthy, dishonest and sneaky.

They're not. The majority of people are decent, law abiding, generous people. Unfortunately, you get to investigate mostly the opposite.

In order to keep some perspective, the following will help:

- Have an active social life outside of the industry. Make sure it's not all work. Hear stories from other people's lives.
- Have a trusted confidant you can talk to or 'download' to. Get things off your chest (without breaching client confidentiality). Externally processing things can be a big help.
- Remain professional and don't get emotionally involved in cases.

Section review (the essentials)

A day in the life of a P.I. isn't all car chases and interviewing people. A lot of it is paperwork, planning and talking to clients. Just remember, almost everything you do will be the result of prior planning. Then once it's done it will require some type of report.

Clients and cases can be separated into personal/domestic cases, and commercial cases. With a bit of creativity, you can find a niche in more uncommon cases as well.

Be careful who you tell once you become a P.I. Also, keep some perspective by having an active social life outside of work, not just within the industry.

Action plan

☐ Have a look through the typical cases. Are there any you'd like to specialize in, or have specific knowledge about? What are some uncommon areas that you know about that you could apply investigative skills to?

☐ Start thinking about who you will/won't tell once you become a private investigator. What will your cover story be? How do you plan on maintaining some work/life separation?

Section 3: Getting work

In this section you will:

- Learn how to (and how not to) approach companies to work for
- Discover the top 3 mistakes people make when looking for a job
- Get some tips on writing a resume
- Find out how to market your own business and get your own cases
- Get an overview on using a website for your business
- Read about the likely jobs you'll get in your first year
- Start thinking about how much to charge

Working for someone, how to get your first role

We've talked about what to expect as a private investigator. You have a rough idea of salary expectations and you've started considering what industries or areas of investigation that interest you.

Now, how do you go about getting that first role?

Remember what I said about the ideal process. It will look something like this:

1. Get your license
2. Start working on your own cases
3. Make yourself a valuable addition to a larger firm
4. Get the experience

If you can't get your license without prior experience, then it changes to this:

1. Make yourself a valuable addition to a larger firm
2. Get the experience
3. Get your license

So, this section is all about getting that first role so you can get some experience. Until you actually start doing the work, everything else is theory. Nothing cements training, education or research more than being given actual work to do.

Remember the two key things that helped me get my first role.

1. Persistence. I called the same company every week for 6 months before they gave me a go.
2. Adding value to their business. Even though I had no investigative experience, I was able to help them with their marketing, systems and website.

The very first step here, before doing anything else, is to see if anyone in your network knows a private investigator. If they do, go and talk to them. It may not be to see if you could work for them, it may just be for a chat. But if you can talk to a real private investigator and ask them the hundreds of questions that I know you have (not at the same time of course), it'll put you on the right track.

You're far more likely to get a meeting with someone you know or share an acquaintance with. I always had a chat to someone who had been referred to me by a friend, purely for the sake of the friend!

If you can't get in touch with a P.I., try a paralegal, lawyer or anyone else in a related field such as security, law enforcement etc.

Make it easy for them to talk to you. It may not be at their office, taking time out of their busy day. They may want you to call them when they're on a long commute, or you could even accompany them on a drive somewhere.

If you don't get a job with them, at least you'll get some great inside information and you can continue your search.

I've seen more people get a job as a P.I. because of who they know, not what they know.

Note, in the US you can get an internship with a licensed private investigation agency. Proof of internship can aid in getting your license. You may be required to intern for 1-2 years depending on which state you're in.

Before going into this just remember that employers already assume one thing. That you are only wanting to work for them to gain experience. Once you've got that experience, you'll start your own company (in competition to them).

They are naturally suspicious, and they need to see what value you can add to them now. If you can help them see exactly how their business would benefit from hiring you than you're well on your way to winning them over. They may want you to sign a confidentiality or non-compete agreement before you start.

You also need to be able to talk to them with a little bit of knowledge on the subject, at least using the correct terminology! This is where your prior research will come into it. Learn the common terms and phrases, have a look at old court records and rulings, and talk to anybody in or closely related to the industry. The more comfortable you are having the conversation, the better you'll come across.

An old case file is absolute gold. If you can read through a few of these you'll know exactly how a P.I. does business, how they manage cases, report to a client and present the report. My first few days as a contractor were spent going through old case files in my spare time. The experience and insight I gained from these was probably better than from any book I read. If you do have a private investigator in your network, ask them if you can read some of their case files (you'll probably have to sign a confidentiality agreement first).

If you can't get a hold of case files, start by looking through publicly available court records. This will give you a good overview of the legal process, how evidence is presented, and how meticulous you need to be.

If you already have a lot of the skills required in this role then you're well ahead of most other candidates. Training someone from scratch is time consuming, time an employer usually doesn't want to spend.

For example, if you can already take good photographs, write a really good report, show great initiative and have demonstrated persistence then you make it easier for them to say yes. If all they have to do is focus your skills, and really just teach you how to be an investigator then their job is mostly done. If you can start on-the-job training straight away, with them knowing that you have the basic skills, you're in a good position.

With the firm you're targeting, have a look at what areas they specialize in. Firstly, ensure that they are the areas that you want to go into, or would like to know more about. Secondly, ensure you pitch your application and skills to those specific areas.

How do you find companies to work for? These days, almost everything is online.

There may or may not be vacancies listed online, depending on where you are and what the market is like. For us in New Zealand, P.I. roles are almost never listed online, they're all filled by word-of-mouth or networking. For larger population centers you'll probably have more luck with job sites.

You'll have a better idea of what online job sites are available in your state. Try putting these into the search bar to see what's available:

- Private investigator
- Surveillance
- Claims investigator
- Process server

Don't be afraid to apply for roles you think you might not have enough experience for. It all depends on what other candidates they have. If there aren't too many applicants, the least you'll get is an interview and that's a foot in the door.

However, ideally you want to skip this process altogether. Sending out resumes, filling out application forms and going to interviews with recruiting agencies can be a huge waste of time (I know, I've done it).

Instead of waiting for roles to come up and then applying for them, why not be top of mind with potential employers when something does become available? This is exactly what I did. Sure, I had to wait six months for something to come up, but it did happen.

If there are job vacancies available, keep applying for them. But don't make this the only thing you're doing. Start calling, visiting and making connections now.

Start with larger firms that have been around for a while. They'll often have more experience in hiring people, more work, and will offer better learning opportunities and support.

The way to find firms is:

- Search online. Most are online, just remember small companies can appear large online, look at the 'about us' and if there's only one person, or no one listed, then it's probably a small company.

- Online directories. Lists of business, e.g. yellow/white pages online.
- Physical directories. this is a good way to tell if someone has been around for a while, look at an older issue, these days it's only larger companies that have been around for a while that list in physical directories.

Before you contact any of them, remember what I said about adding value to them. The first contact you make with them should not be about what they can do for you, it should be what you can do for them. Show them that you've researched them, know about their company, and can help them in specific areas.

Small companies can also be good, depending on what stage of growth they're at. If you see them in a media a lot, or they appear to have invested in advertising/marketing then it's likely that they're growing. They will be more open to hiring someone who can help them grow.

In most cases, employers will want you to contract to them (so they don't have to pay you unless you're actually working on a case). This is quite standard across the industry. So, you'll want to set yourself up in business first. Requirements vary between states and countries, so I won't go into too much detail here. Basically, you need to be ready to legally work as a private investigator, whether in your own business or for someone else.

As far as naming your business goes, some countries require that you operate under your own name. I don't see this as a bad thing, it saves calling yourself 'Ace Investigations' or similar (there are thousands out there like that). It also sets you off in the right mindset. If you're doing something in your own name, you'll want to do a good job.

Remember, when deciding on your name, email address, website, business cards etc. keep two things in mind. Be consistent and be professional.

With regards to insurance, if you are doing your own cases you will need insurance, at least public liability. If you are contracting to someone else, their insurance in most cases will cover you. But don't just assume, ask them if it does or not (it will be written in the contract). When choosing your own insurance, I strongly suggest that you talk to a broker who specializes or has significant experience in providing insurance for private investigators.

Now that I've been on the other side for a while (having people call me wanting to become a P.I.) I have a pretty good idea of what works and what doesn't.

Remember what I said before about prospective employers. Their default answer is 'no'. Do any of the following three things and you make it that much easier for them to say no.

1. Saying you're enthusiastic, keen and a quick learner, without any evidence.

If you say these things, but have no actions to back them up, they're not only redundant, they're a complete lie. Every single person who has contacted me has said these words. I can only think of one person who actually had the evidence. She got a job with us.

How enthusiastic and keen are you? Have you contacted them more than once? Do you contact them weekly to let them know you're still keen? Have you already got your license by yourself? Have you started working on cases, real or practice?

Have you taken a real interest in their business, have you identified some specific areas where you could help? Can you show how your past experience could increase their business or make things easier for them?

Have you started learning by yourself? How many books have you read? How many courses have you been on? Have you asked them if you could tag along on some cases to get a better idea of them?

By all means, say these things. But you'd better provide plenty of evidence to back them up.

2. Saying you'll work for free.

Nothing appears more desperate than offering to work for free. And the very last thing you want to appear as is desperate.

A way to not appear desperate is this: Instead of thinking 'how can they help me, I really need them', think 'how can I help them, what value do I have to add, what areas do they need me in'. This is true in every negotiation. The person who has more to offer and isn't as desperate generally gets what they want. You may not have more to offer them, but at least don't act like you've got nothing to offer.

Saying you'll work for free also says that you don't value your work. If you don't value it, why should they?

If a firm asks you to work for free that's a slightly different case but would need to be evaluated carefully. In my experience, no reputable firm will ask you this. Anything they do they will be charging a client for. If they're charging the client, they should be paying you.

Yes, there are genuine (rare) situations where they couldn't charge a client for your time, but this should be the exception not the rule. They may want an unpaid trial period which could be suitable. Just ensure that each party knows exactly what to expect, when the trial period will end, and what new conditions will take its place.

3. Not being professional.

Private investigation is a client-facing, service-based business. As such, everything you do needs to appear professional. This is important not only because it ensures things are done correctly and in order, but it also helps bring in business. Who would you rather use, someone who appears professional or unprofessional?

The firm that you're talking to has a brand and reputation to uphold. They're not going to allow an unprofessional contractor or employee damage that. Therefore, your emails, letters, business cards, phone conversations and appearance need to show them that they could trust you with their work.

Spelling or grammar mistakes, missed appointments and an unprofessional attitude will almost certainly get them to say no.

Writing a resume or CV

This is a huge area and there are so many free online resources around that I won't even begin to scratch the surface on this one.

On top of what you can find online, here are some P.I. specific tips:

- Investigative business owners or managers are busy people. They don't have time to read a book on you. Keep it to 1-2 pages. The aim is to get them to want to know more, not to tell them everything in one go.
- Don't say you've always wanted to be a spy. It's ok to say you've always wanted to be a P.I., explain why you didn't and the 'responsible' things that you did in the meantime.
- If you've had lots of jobs in the past, don't list them all. Especially if it makes it look like you can't actually stick at one thing. Try to categorize them. I.e. worked in hospitality 2009-2013 instead of listing the 7 different employers you worked for.
- Make sure your resume shows that you have the key attributes to become a P.I. Communication skills, common sense, persistence, professionalism, confidence.

Remember I said that it pays to start developing your own cases first, before you approach a larger firm to work for? There are several ways to do this and I'll outline them here.

It starts with knowing where a lot of work comes from.

Law firms

Whether you're working for yourself getting your first few cases, or if you're working for someone else, the most common source of cases is from lawyers, paralegals, attorneys or solicitors. Lawyers are busy people so they're very willing to delegate work to someone who is keen to take it, someone they can trust to get the job done correctly.

When I first started out, I sent a letter to all the local law firms in my area. I then followed up with a call, and then finally I paid them a visit (most of the time it was a quick handshake, and a reminder to keep me in mind – they don't have time for much more). This is actually how I got most of my work initially.

Before you can do this, you need to make sure that you have your branding and stationery sorted. It needs to look professional and consistent. Yes, you may be working out of a spare room in your house initially, but you want an attorney to look at it and think 'professional' not 'cheap'. There's nothing wrong with appearing like a small firm or owner/operator, but you still need to look like you take your job seriously.

Giving a follow up call and a visit shows them that you're persistent (a great attribute every P.I. needs to have) and that you are eager to work. Lawyers are always busy, and when they need something done by a P.I. they'll pick the first one that comes to mind. You may not be able to break into a firm that has used the same P.I. for years, but there are plenty of new lawyers who are using a P.I. for the first time. If they remember you because you sent them something, called them and visited them then you'll be top of mind.

I usually approached the smaller firms as larger ones tend to have regular investigators that they use. That being said, keep in mind that it's often up to the individual attorney to arrange their own P.I. So, if you're targeting a larger firm, make sure you pick a specific person to target and include their name on correspondence. This will make sure it goes to them and doesn't get thrown away at reception.

Another great tactic is to include an actual example case file, with your surveillance notes, report, video footage etc. (an example – not a real case!). Show them everything you can do. Spend some time on this and more often than not it will be a lot better than what they're receiving from their current private investigator. Either that, or they've never used a private investigator, and, from your report, they can see how much it would help them. Impress them and they'll want that sort of work on their next case.

Some report resources and examples are:

https://investigatormarketing.com/shop/
http://pursuitmag.com/writing-the-perfect-investigative-report/

Don't oversell yourself either. There is no point saying you can do all types of investigations when you can't as this will just come back to bite you. Be honest and be prepared to prove yourself doing the simpler tasks such as serving documents and traces.

As a matter of fact, when it comes to marketing, the more targeted you can be the better. For example, if you say you do 'all types of investigations' someone reading that can't relate it to a specific case they're working on right now. However, if you say you do 'process serving' or 'tracing' then that relates to a specific instance where they can use you. In marketing, more is not better, targeted is better.

An even better way is to tell stories. Tell them what problems a client had and how you solved them. The more relatable the better. Get them thinking about how you can help them too.

A lot of these cases will be for a fixed fee. Be prepared to win some and lose some. You may find the person, or complete the document service in ten minutes, or it may take hours. Don't say no to work from lawyers. If you want to build a good relationship with them be prepared to take some hits on the harder cases.

Insurance companies

These can be a little harder to get work from, especially when starting out. They are desirable clients for everyone. From the guy that's just started up, to the large firm that's been going for 40 years. This is because there's always a steady supply of work, they pay in full and on time, and they are not afraid to spend money to get a result.

On the flip side, they expect results and reports quickly, they expect professionalism (they have a brand to protect) and they are often the ones who set the rates, not you.

There are a few different types of investigations for insurance companies. Worker's compensation fraud, personal injury, vehicle crash or accident investigations and loss or theft investigations.

There are many more specific areas as well, but they can generally be separated into two groups or aims. One is to establish whether the insured is at fault, or whether someone else is responsible (therefore someone else has to cover it). The second is to establish whether the insured is telling the truth on their claim or not.

Yes, the aim of the insurance company is to find out whether they need to pay the claim or not. And you may not be comfortable with that. However, your job is solely to report on the facts. In my experience, the cases tended to be fairly black and white. Either the claimant had clearly lied when submitting their claim, and the insurance company didn't pay. Or, there was no evidence to suggest that they had lied, everything pointed to them telling the truth and the insurance company paid.

A lot of the larger firms use their own inhouse investigators, however even they will use private investigators in certain areas or when the workload is heavy.

If you have prior experience in a particular field, then you may be able to target this niche in the insurance investigations area. For example, I know someone who started out as a fireman, became a P.I. and now makes a decent living investigating house fires for insurance companies. I also know someone who worked as a vehicle accident investigator in the police force. He now works as the same but contracting to insurance companies (and he makes twice as much as he did in the police force).

County indigent defense programs

In the US, this is the state sponsored defense program that ensures each defendant in court has access to a public defender, even if they can't afford it. The program employs or appoints attorneys to represent the defendants. Most countries have a similar program.

There is usually a list of licensed private investigators that can be instructed by the court or requested by the individual attorney to work on each particular case. To get on this list you usually need to be vetted by the program.

If you wish to work in the defense program you need to firstly get on the list, and secondly build good relationships with the appointed attorneys. If you have a good relationship with them, they'll generally want to use you again on their other cases.

Not only that, when these young attorneys start their own practice or begin working for someone else, they'll want to continue to use the private investigator who they know will get the job done.

Government agencies

Another common source is from state, federal or government agencies. Often these require further vetting to work on them, but they are a steady source of income once you're in.

Most larger government contracts are tied up by large investigative or legal firms, however there are still opportunities in this area. Try some of the smaller departments who wouldn't necessarily be a target client for a large firm. Also keep an eye on recent law changes. The need for a P.I. because of increased workload or a new direction/department opening up is also an opportunity.

Social media

Before we talk about advertising on social media, there's something you need to do first. You need to make sure that your professional and personal social media profiles are kept completely separate. And that your personal profiles are 100% private. The reason for this should be obvious.

As a P.I. you will deal with people who will definitely have cause to hold a grudge. You may be directly involved in them going to prison, losing their job, losing their criminal proceeds etc. These are often the types of people who have a bit of time on their hands and will think of ways to get back at you.

If you have a Facebook account, there are various privacy settings. When I was working on higher risk cases I had mine set almost at the highest level. People could still find my name if they searched for me (so legitimate friends could still find and add me) but you couldn't see any information about me at all if you weren't a friend. No photos, no likes, no posts, no cities or contact details. The same goes for all other forms of social media. Take your safety seriously, including that of your family.

Some good links are:
https://identity.utexas.edu/everyone/how-to-manage-your-social-media-privacy-settings
https://socialpilot.co/blog/ultimate-guide-manage-social-media-privacy-settings/

Once you've done that, you can move on to setting up new profiles for your business. I won't go into too much detail as there are plenty of articles and books about using social media for your business. However, I'll give a brief overview.

The first and most obvious accounts to create would be LinkedIn and Facebook. If used correctly, LinkedIn is a great way to connect with business owners and other professionals. The ones that will likely be needing the services of a P.I. for commercial jobs. Facebook on the other hand tends to be more useful for smaller businesses owners and domestic/personal clients. Both platforms offer the ability to run advertisements, which can be very targeted and therefore more cost effective than say Google AdWords. Although Google is catching up with Facebook as far as targeting goes. I've personally used Facebook ads with a great success rate.

The approach to take is very similar to trying to get your first role with an investigative company. What value can I add to this person or organization? What do they need right now? Start asking lots of questions and try to put yourself in their shoes. Once you've come up with that you can then start creating content and ads that serve those needs. What particular words will grab them? For example, instead of saying 'Private Investigation Services Available', address a particular need. I.e. 'Need a document served quick smart – call me now', or 'Think your spouse is cheating on you – I can check for you'.

The more specific and targeted, the better and more qualified the response will be.

Obviously, privacy is key, so don't expect people to 'like' your page or posts as they won't want other people to see that necessarily. Most people don't like to advertise the fact that they need a P.I. Instead aim to make it easy for them to contact you confidentially.

Blogging can also be useful, but this is something you need to constantly update, and it's a long-term strategy. It will not give instant results. The key is to create content that is actually helpful and gives value now, without them having to even use your services yet. If they feel like they've been given something valuable for free they'll be more inclined to use you in the future. It could be something as simple as a guide such as '10 signs that your spouse may be cheating on you', or '5 ways to do your own background check on a potential employee'. It's great if you can give them some initial steps to take, and then of course call you when they need some more specific help.

Some further links for social media marketing:
https://investigatormarketing.com/social-media-private-investigators/
http://pursuitmag.com/social-media-marketing-for-pis/
https://www.linkedin.com/pulse/7-social-media-tips-private-investigators-chet-engstrom

Using your network and referrals

The one technique that can pay the most dividends quickly is using your own personal and professional network. This is usually an under-appreciated avenue of work and yet it can be the easiest to get results from. How often do you need something done and trust a recommendation from a friend a lot more than any advertising or online research? It's human nature, we're inclined to trust someone if we know someone else who trusts them.

So, the first step would be let everyone your contacts know that you're a private investigator. In a non-pushy and authentic way. For your closer friends, you will have no doubt discussed this at length so they'll already know. It may take the form of an email to your extended family, and you might slowly get the word out each time you catch up with everybody else. It helps to have a stack of business cards to give them. That way when they do come across someone to refer you to, they don't have to hunt around looking for your phone number or email address (or end up giving out your personal details).

Even if you only have 200 people that you associate with or come across regularly (most people have around 500: 150 socially, 350 from other circles), and those 200 each have 200 they associate with, that's 40,000 people that you can be recommended to! And you won't just be a random name or company to them, you'll be someone they will tend to trust because you have a mutual acquaintance.

The second step is to educate your friends on just what a private investigator can be used for. When you say 'private investigator' to most people they think of infidelity or divorce cases. Start talking about the other cases you've done or heard of. Pretty soon they'll realize that there are a lot of uses for investigators. And they're more likely than not to come across someone who needs one.

Also remember to always ask for referrals. If you're doing a good job you shouldn't be embarrassed or afraid to ask for a referral. Lawyers talk to other lawyers, and if they're happy with your work they'll want to tell other people about it! Sometimes they just need a reminder.

A lot of businesses work solely on referrals. And in New Zealand (being a small country), most work that larger investigative firms get is through word of mouth.

Website

Every business needs a website. It is your online presence and is often the first thing people will see. These days there are plenty of programs and platforms that allow you to build one yourself. This may be an option if you're fairly technically savvy and have a good eye for detail. If you're not, then there are other paid options.

I won't go into any detail here on building your website or getting it built, as the internet is full of good free advice on this. As a quick note, I built my own website through WordPress, and have built a number of WordPress websites since then.

You may not necessarily get a lot of business through your website (which I'll talk about soon) but it is another brick in building trust with your clients. If they see that you have a professional website, and are able to find out more about what you do, before talking to you, they'll be a better qualified lead when they finally pick up the phone and call you.

Think of it as a representative of you or your business, out there in the world, constantly representing you.

As far as getting new business goes, a website only works if people can find it. It's the same for physical stores. If you're tucked down some side street and haven't told anyone where you are, your walk-in traffic is going to be very small. It pays to think of a website not as marketing or advertising in itself, but as the destination that all your advertising points to.

So, make sure you have your website listed on all your business cards, flyers and correspondence. Then you can use other methods such as Facebook advertising, Google AdWords and any other traditional forms (radio, TV, mailouts) to point people to your website.

Think of your website like the hub at the center of a wheel. This is where you want everyone to eventually end up. Everything else is like the spokes. They're all pointing to the center. If someone finds you on Facebook, or hears about you on the radio, you want them to end up at your website as this is the platform you have complete control over.

You also will want a good SEO (search engine optimization) strategy. This is the strategy used to get your website ranked higher in search engines such as Google, Bing etc. Even if you can build your own website, I would suggest using a paid service for this. Your website host can usually offer this, and prices start at a few dollars per month.

You can also engage a third-party company to do it. Prices and results vary but I have, at various times, spent a few hundred dollars per month on this. Just make sure that you are getting results. A good technique when choosing a company is to Google 'SEO' and the city that you're targeting. For example, if you want to get your website ranking higher for people in Houston, then Google 'SEO Houston'. Obviously the first (non-paid) results will be the companies that are the best at it!

I have also used SEO experts through task sites such as Upwork, an online freelancer platform. Be selective in who you choose as it can be done badly.

Ideally, choose someone with lots of good references and examples of previous successful jobs.

Remember, your website is often the first thing people see. So, make it engaging and be very specific about who you're targeting with it.

Associations and P.I. directories

There may be a dedicated P.I. association you can join depending on where you are. It may even be a broader investigator and security association. This can be useful for a few reasons. They may offer business and investigative help, seminars and tools. It can also be a good chance to make contacts with larger firms (especially when looking for your first role). You may get leads through it as people sometimes go directly to associations with their case, for recommendations. It can also add trust to your brand.

An association that I belong to is very active in pursuing its own links with various industry groups. As a result, we get a lot of leads and requests through this association. So, check what sort of links with industry the association has.

There are also plenty of local business groups that you can join. Try to think about what groups your target market may belong to. Even shared interests such as sports or hobbies can allow you to network. Again, make sure you're not pushy and are being authentic. You have to be genuinely interested in the sport and not just be there for the networking!

Rotary, business breakfast groups, Meetups, civic groups and whatever other groups are out there can all be useful. Just remember the old adage, you get out what you put in. If you want to network, you need to be there in person to network, not just have your name on the membership list.

Be careful with P.I. directories, or online directories in general. There are countless out there. For most, their main goal is to pressure you into paying for a higher ranking on their platform. As a rule, I never paid for any directory listings. Most people use online search engines instead. If you've never heard of the directory and have never used it, chances are no one else has.

By all means, get a free listing on there (it may help your search engine ranking) but don't pay for it.

Conventions

Conventions and conferences can work really well if targeted correctly. Identify your target market and pick a convention where you think the highest number of those people and companies will be. They can be tiring, as you're talking to a lot of people in a short amount of time, but the leads you get from it can be invaluable. It's your chance to physically put yourself in front of people who may need a private investigator.

If you're working for someone else, there are several jobs that they'll most likely start you on. Ones where they can see how you do, with little risk of blowing the case. These are great for experience and a good chance to prove yourself to your employer.

This is also an opportunity for the new P.I. with no experience. Since many investigators come from law enforcement, the last thing they want to do when making the career change to a private investigator is these cases. They just want to sink their teeth into a nice, long, complex investigation.

So, there are plenty of cases you can pick up that no experienced investigator wants to do. It can be great billing for your employer, and if you apply yourself with focus and gusto, they'll just keep feeding you more and more complex cases.

A great place to be in the eyes of your new employer is someone who is always available and will always approach each case with enthusiasm. Someone who actually thinks for themselves and doesn't just go through the process.

This is how I very quickly became the preferred agent for the company I worked for. Put yourself in the shoes of your employer. They have dozens of cases on the go, they want to be able to allocate them to someone they can trust to get the job done. Be that person and they'll have your number on speed dial.

As a side note, if you get given a task you're not quite sure about or comfortable with, do not try and bluff your way through it! Always ask questions first. There is nothing wrong with admitting you may need some help, and you'll find people are generally more than willing to help you.

As long as you don't ask the same questions twice (I always took notes when asking for advice) then they'll be happy to answer. Remember, if you make a mistake it can cost the company a client. Better to ask first, you and the company you're working for have a business to protect.

These are some of the cases you'll probably be given:

- Worker's claims investigation, mostly surveillance, you'll progress to the investigative side later

- Reviewing and reporting on surveillance footage, either from CCTV, other agent's photos and videos etc.
- Conducting background checks, searching databases and records
- Process service or document service, locating someone and ensuring they get handed some documents personally
- Repossessions and debt collection (if you work for a firm that does these, it may require a separate license)
- Taking witness statements, you'll progress to full interviews later

Remember, everything that you do will eventually end up in a report. The end of the day is usually always taken up with writing a job sheet or report. Keeping good field notes as you go is crucial. I pretend I have a terrible memory and so I have to write everything down, this is a good tactic. There are only so many things you can remember in a day.

Furthermore, you may end up in court two years later, as a witness for the prosecution or defense. There is nothing worse than being cross-examined by the opposing counsel and you realize that you should have kept better notes. I know. I've been there. You only make that mistake once.

Not only that, a lot of jobs can lead to other things. I.e. a simple document service might turn into a trace. Therefore, it's important to approach every job as if it's the start of something bigger. Take copious notes keeping in mind what further action may be required. You may have to go back to those notes again.

This is a tricky one. Many people will say that when you start out you should be undercutting your competition and getting as much work as you can. Just as many people say that you should charge higher fees because then you've got an incentive to do really great work, and people tend to value something if they pay more for it.

I tend towards the latter. However, it's not really fair to be charging a high price when you don't have much experience. So, when starting out I tended to keep my rates around what everybody else charged but offered a much better (and more personalized) service. I did the best work I could, hoping for referrals rather than a huge volume of work initially.

I also stopped charging if I had made a mistake (i.e. spent an hour following the wrong lead). Clients shouldn't have to pay for your learning experiences.

As I got more experience, my rates went up. And because I had good referrals people were willing to pay more.

Investigators can charge a client anywhere from $35 to $150 an hour or more, depending on their level of experience, training or expertise.

Be clear about your hourly rate, but you should also charge what it's worth to your client, not what it costs you. For example, if you're an expert in a particular area you can charge a lot higher rates. You've worked hard to become an expert so you should be rewarded for that. Your services are also very valuable to a client because they either couldn't do it themselves or it would take a lot longer. Just make sure you are delivering that professional service that's worth the fee to them.

Of course, you don't have to worry about any of this if you get a role as a contractor/agent with a larger firm. They will set the rates and you don't have much of an option. That's why it pays to go for a role with a reputable firm, not one that is only interested in turnover and burns its agents.

Remember, you charge for any work that you do. You don't charge only for successful results (as you can't guarantee that). As soon as you accept a client's instructions you're charging for your time and expenses. This includes phone calls, vehicle use, emailing, researching, reporting. And if your client is a private (domestic) client, get payment up front.

It is also commonly accepted to charge your client for any time spent in court, even if you are summoned by the opposing counsel.

Section review (the essentials):

See if anyone in your network knows a private investigator. If they do, go and talk to them. It may not be to see if you could work for them, it may just be for a chat. But if you can talk to a real private investigator it'll put you on the right track.

Ensure you approach any prospective employer showing them clearly how they could benefit from employing you. Show them what you can do for them, not just want you want them to do for you. What value can you add now?

Cover all bases. Don't just apply for jobs online and hope for the best. Start talking to people, visiting firms and making contacts.

Don't say you're enthusiastic, keen and a quick learner without any evidence. Don't say that you'll work for free. Always be professional. Be persistent.

Write a resume that gets the reader wanting to know more. Ensure it demonstrates that you have communication skills, common sense, persistence, professionalism and confidence.

Good sources of work are law firms, insurance companies, county indigent defense programs and government agencies.

Use social media to your advantage. Also explore your network and get referrals, this is an underappreciated yet high value avenue for work.

Your website is an extension of your business. Often it is the first thing people will see. Ensure it matches who you're targeting and what you specialize in.

A great place to be in the eyes of your new employer is someone who is always available, will always approach each case with enthusiasm and someone who thinks for themselves.

Action plan:

☐   Find someone in your network (friend of a friend etc.) that you can talk to. Ideally a private investigator, or someone in a closely related field.

Weak ties and networking trump cold calling any day of the week. Start looking now, start talking to people now.

☐ Search the common online job sites in your area. Put the following into the search field: private investigator, surveillance, claims investigator, process server. See what comes up.

☐ With the list of firms you identified in one of the previous sections, start calling and visiting them. Make some contacts there. They may not be looking for someone now, but stay top of mind for when they are.

☐ Start working on your resume. Look online for a template that suits you. Make it P.I. specific, ensuring you show that you have the attributes to be a great P.I.

☐ Identify any industry specific conventions and conferences that may be suitable for you to attend.

The following action points are only applicable if you are able to get your license and begin working on your own cases:

☐ Make a list of all law firms in your area. Send every single one an introduction letter, follow it up with a phone call, and then visit all of them. The same goes with insurance companies. Ensure your correspondence, and corporate identity is consistent and professional.

☐ Contact the office responsible for your county indigent defense program. See what you need to do to get on their list of approved private investigators.

☐ Identify local state, federal or government agencies. Find out if any of them use private investigators. If they do, talk to the person responsible for instructing the investigators. See what you need to do to become approved.

☐ Develop a social media plan. What platforms will you be on? What does your target audience use? What tips, guides and articles can you write now? Set up your social media profiles now.

- [ ] Build a website now. Even if you don't have much to put on it yet, set it up. Before you do, answer these two questions: Who are you targeting with it? How are you solving their problems? Be specific, you need to be able to engage your audience as soon as they arrive.

- [ ] List your company on every suitable local directory you can find. At this stage only set up a free listing.

Section 4: The next steps – preparation

In this section you will:

- Start preparing yourself for a job as a private investigator
- Sort out your finances
- Think about how you will handle rejection
- Find out how to start doing practice investigations
- Decide on your values, ethics and integrity now

Get your finances sorted

It doesn't take a lot of money to set yourself up in business as a P.I. The most expensive outlay is the equipment but if you do your research or buy second-hand then you can save on that too. It also doesn't require large overheads. You don't have to rent an office if you don't want to, and the type of car you use can be very similar or the same as the one you're driving now.

The biggest cost by far, is the lost income (or opportunity cost). By this I mean the income you could have earned by staying in your current job (or starting work immediately in whatever job you can get), instead of working on your P.I. business. Whether that's building the investigative business that you've started or trying to get your first role working for someone else.

This can take months. Remember, it took me six months before I started getting a regular paycheck. So, you have two basic options.

The first (and probably best) option is to have a side business that can support you, I've talked about this earlier in the book. Something that provides you regular income to at least pay the bills, and something you can drop once things get busy as a P.I.

The second is to remain in your current job while working nights and weekends to become a P.I. Be aware that it's more difficult to focus on one thing while trying to do a good job in a full-time occupation though.

If neither of these options suit you then you need to ensure you have the cash to support you while you're not working. Enough until you start getting those regular cases.

How long? It really depends on where you are. New Zealand is a tough place to find work as a P.I. so we would be at the longer end of the scale. If you're in a large city with plenty of private investigative agencies, then you might not need to wait that long. You'll get a better idea once you start reading and talking to people in your particular area.

So, in short, make sure you have enough funding or other work to support you for 6-12 months.

Commit to it and don't take no for an answer

Another title for this section could have been 'how to handle rejection'. Starting something new is an amazing, yet daunting, experience. You're eager to learn and you're excited Yet there is the other side to that. Feeling out of your depth, vulnerable and powerless.

How do you balance the need to talk to as many people as possible, with the absolute certainty that you will face rejection and even some discouragement?

There is no easy answer for this. There are plenty of resources that cover this topic, I would suggest reading some articles or books by Tony Robbins or similar.

Some quick suggestions or tips that helped me:

- Plan for rejection because you will get it. It's rare that you get the first job that you apply for. Don't take it personally, use it as a way to refine your interviewing and presentation skills. For every 'no' that you get, ask for feedback and then work on those specific points. If anything, it's a quick way to find out what areas you're lacking in and how you can improve.

- On that point, don't apply for the company you really want to work for first. Practice with other companies and interviews until you feel confident that you'll nail the interview that counts.

- Don't take no as your final answer. Imagine that there are a certain amount of 'no's' that you need to get before a yes comes along. No one knows how many there need to be, so just keep trying until you eventually get that yes.

- Commit to doing this. If you're going to do this, you can't think 'I'll give it a go and if it gets too hard, I'll give up and try something else'. That's a sure-fire way to fail, it gives you an easy out. Really picture yourself as a private investigator and you'll have no choice but to find a way to become one.

- Limit who you tell. Some people will support you and some will discourage you. If this is something you really want to do, you need people who will support you. That said, getting good feedback from

71

people who know you well is essential. For example, if you couldn't answer those questions in the section on 'why you shouldn't become a private investigator' then maybe you need some good, honest feedback from a trusted confidant first.

Remember, persistence is one of the most important qualities as a private investigator. If you can't persist in becoming a P.I., what makes you think you'll have enough persistence to actually do the work?

Start investigating now (doing practice investigations)

Just because you don't have any paying clients yet doesn't mean that you can't start doing the work. Like most things in life, you can read all you want, but you don't know what it's really like until you start doing it.

So, start doing practice investigations. Give yourself a scenario (pick one of the common cases we've already mentioned) and get to work. Do everything you think you might come across during that investigation, including the report (you can use it as your sample report to send to lawyers).

Ask your friends if they have a scenario for you. They might have a real case that you could practice on!

Start practicing vehicle tailing (you'll soon realize how hard it is). Pick a vehicle and see if you can follow it for a short while, without ever being the car directly behind it. Just tail it for a little while then break off. You don't want to scare some unsuspecting motorist because you're new at it, and it's obvious that you're following them!

Read as many articles on it as you like, but then get in your car and start following people. The good thing about tailing is you do make quick progress once you start doing it. I was entirely self-taught when I started tailing people. It wasn't until I had been successfully working for a while that I finally got some informal training from an experienced surveillance operative.

Remember, the objective isn't to conduct a perfect investigation. It's to provide a realistic training exercise that you can use to identify areas you need to work on or read more about.

Another very important skill is taking notes. As I've said before, everything will end up in a report (often written a day or more later) so accurate notes are crucial. Ideally, you'll have a dedicated voice recorder (not just on your phone, a separate one). That way you can record detailed notes as you're driving.

Develop your written note taking too. You'll very quickly come up with your own abbreviations and acronyms to suit your style of writing. Also experiment with note taking apps on your phone. In certain situations (like in a café) when you can't use a voice recorder and taking written notes would look suspicious, you'll need to take notes on your phone. Nothing as innocent as someone in a café on their phone, everyone does it these days!

Get familiar with social media and internet searches. The amount of free information available, showing you exactly how everything works, is astonishing. Start reading the articles and experimenting.

Here's a good article from Google on how to refine web searches:

https://support.google.com/websearch/answer/2466433?hl=en

This can also help you in your actual search for a job.

Decide on your values, ethics and integrity now

This is the last section in the book, and it covers one of the most important topics. One that will affect the rest of your career as a private investigator.

As a private investigator you deal with dishonesty, lack of integrity, blurred moral boundaries and illegal activity. How do you deal with that without it affecting how you operate?

You decide on your values now.

Decide now as to exactly what you will and won't do in certain situations. Develop scenarios and exercises and decide now what your instant reaction will be.

If you go into this line of work with no clear boundaries, then you can get into trouble very easily.

Your reputation and your business depend on you having clear and unwavering integrity.

Don't ever compromise this for the sake of a client, more money or a successful outcome. Clients, money and cases come and go. Once your integrity and reputation is publicly tarnished, it's very hard to build it up again.

Here are some principals to stick to:

- Do not ever state something in court that you know to be incorrect. If in doubt, say 'I don't know' and stick to it no matter how much the opposing counsel pushes. Whilst not ideal, appearing unsure is much better than committing perjury (willfully telling an untruth or misrepresentation under oath). For things that could be argued, get into the habit of saying 'it appeared to me that...'. No one can argue how it appeared to you.

- Pretexts. Pretexting is giving a reason for doing something that is not the real reason. Or more simply, not telling the whole truth. In most cases this is not illegal, and there definitely are times where pretexting is the only option. What would you say when a neighbor of someone you're watching knocks on your car window at 1am wondering what you're doing? Of course, you're not going to give the real reason. However, never imply or state that you are a police officer, government employee, representative of a legal department or anybody else acting in an official capacity. This is simply illegal and you should never jeopardize your freedom or ability to continue working. When getting people to talk to you, some creativity is required. Stick as close to the truth as possible. It's easier to remember that way, and you'll come across more naturally.

- One day you'll be in a social situation and someone will find out that you're a private investigator. Then the questions and stories will follow. When telling stories (which you definitely will do), never reveal who was involved, whether a company or person. Ensure that information remains confidential. By all means, tell all the stories you want. Just ensure you never break client confidentiality. Use generalizations. In fact, after those particularly interesting cases that you know will make good stories, decide then how you're going to tell it to ensure there are no breaches or slips of the tongue.

- What about when people ask for legal advice, whether a client, someone you're interviewing or just an acquaintance. It's tempting to pretend you're an expert, since you know slightly more about it than the next person. However, as a private investigator, you are not a lawyer. You don't get paid to give people legal advice, and the advice you give may well be incorrect. You don't want that responsibility. Recommend a lawyer instead (preferably one who gives you work, so you can return the favor).

- Don't take things personally. Your client, the person you're interviewing and whomever else you deal with may (and probably will) take things personally. Don't fall into that trap yourself. Don't get emotionally involved as we all know that decisions made because of emotion are seldom the best decisions.

- You will make mistakes. If you can fix them yourself without anyone knowing, all well and good. If they come to light, or if they are going to affect the case, own them, take responsibility and do what you can to fix them. Don't ever lie or blame someone else when it comes to mistakes. People will respect you for it in the long run, and it's another way to learn and improve.

- Don't inflate the bill for the client just because you can, and don't charge for work that you didn't do.

- Don't lie on your report, whether it's for the sake of a good outcome, or to cover a potential mistake. For example, you will lose sight of people you're following. Plenty of times in your career. It may be because you made a mistake, lost concentration or for reasons outside of your control. Don't make up some elaborate story as to how they got away. Simply state that you lost sight of them, and the steps you took to try and regain sight.

- On rare occasions, you may be asked to spy on a competitor for someone. This is known as corporate espionage. There are some investigators who focus solely on this. It's a murky world, one where you run very close to the legal line. As a business owner myself, I would hate the fact that a competitor got the upper hand by spying and potentially stealing my ideas. So, I wouldn't take on this type of investigation. Competitor analysis is one thing, stealing their secrets is another. Would you take on this case?

- More often, you'll be asked if you can hack someone's phone or computer. This is simply illegal. Don't do it, even if you are smart enough to.

- Don't break the law. Sounds simple, but it can be tempting, especially when the case isn't going your way. Keep on the right side of privacy laws, trespass laws, wiretapping, GPS etc. Know your state laws. Ignorance is not a defense. Remember, plan for most cases to end up in court. Do you want your methods to be scrutinized by a judge?

- Get liability insurance, and errors and omissions insurance. Mistakes happen, and some can be serious. Protect yourself.

Think of some other situations you may find yourself in. How will you respond? What values do you hold now that you won't compromise?

Remember, being a private investigator can be hugely rewarding. However, often you're dealing with other people's problems and situations. Situations you would never dream of getting yourself into. You may even think that it's their fault, and that no outcome is really going to be good.

Solving the case may not feel rewarding to you. In that case, knowing that you did a really good job is your reward. Knowing that you applied yourself, did the best you could and didn't compromise your integrity should be all you need.

Think long term and treat others how you'd like to be treated.

Section review (the essentials):

It can take months before you start getting work as a P.I. Make sure you have enough funding or other work to support you for 6-12 months.

Be prepared for rejection and discouragement. It will happen. Keep going, stay committed and don't take no for an answer.

Start doing practice investigations. Nothing cements theory or identifies areas for improvement than getting out there and doing it.

As a private investigator you deal with dishonesty, lack of integrity, blurred moral boundaries and illegal activity. How do you deal with that without it affecting how you operate? You decide on your values now.

Action plan:

☐   Make sure you have enough funding or other work to support you for 6-12 months. Work out how much you spend in 12 months and either have at least this amount available, or a guaranteed source of income to cover it.

☐   If you need to, get some honest feedback about your decision to become a P.I. from someone you respect and trust.

☐   Plan for rejection now. How are you going to handle it? How can you get valuable feedback from each person that says no?

☐   Start doing practice investigations. Pick a scenario or ask your friends for a real one. Do everything including writing the report. This can be used as an example report that you send to prospective clients.

☐   Get liability and errors and omissions insurance.

☐   Your integrity is everything. Decide how you'll act in certain situations now.

Closing

Well done for making it this far. It shows that you are taking this seriously and that you have one of the most important traits you'll need – persistence!

You now have a lot more information than I had when I first started out. There doesn't seem to be a lot of information for people with little or no experience, I struggled to find anything written by someone with a similar background to me (non-law enforcement). I wished there was a book like this, which is the exact reason why I wrote it.

But information is worthless without action.

While the process appears simple (which it is), it is certainly not easy. Like most things in life, there are no shortcuts to becoming a private investigator. I can't do it for you, I can only point you in the right direction. The rest is up to you. It will take hard work, persistence and an underlying desire that you do really want to become a private investigator.

There may be days, weeks where you don't seem to be making any progress. Remember, it took me six months before I finally got a role with an investigative firm.

Keep going and believe that you will make it. When things come easy you don't tend to value them as much. Think about a great achievement in your life that you really value. I can guarantee that it wasn't easy either.

All that said, the information you now have will help you considerably in knowing where to focus your efforts. It will save you hours of work, trial and error and will allow you to start your process with confidence. Confidence knowing it can be done, and the reality check of knowing that it may not be easy.

I sincerely hope that you have enjoyed this book, but more importantly, have found it useful. The whole reason for writing this book is to help people like you to become a P.I., so if you have any feedback, I would love to hear from you. You can email me at hello@kurt.nz

Also, if you have found the book useful please leave a review. They help more than you think.

I wish you all the best for your journey ahead.

Sincerely,

Kurt Breetvelt

Resources and links

Some links may have moved or changed. For a full and up-to-date list visit:

www.kurt.nz/pibook

Note: The resources and links listed are only suggested as sources for further exploration. They do not imply endorsement or guarantee accuracy of the information they contain.

How other people became a private investigator

A classroom teacher discovers her love of criminal justice and finds her perfect job.
http://pursuitmag.com/how-became-private-investigator/

A Florida private investigator explains how she learned the tricks of her trade: by catching shoplifters
http://pursuitmag.com/private-investigator-start-loss-prevention/

10 skills journalism brings to private investigations work
http://pursuitmag.com/10-skills-journalism-private-investigations-work/

Q&A: Mike Spencer, Bay Area private investigator
http://pursuitmag.com/mike-spencer-bay-area-private-investigator/

Career spotlight: what I do as a private investigator
https://www.lifehacker.com.au/2016/04/career-spotlight-what-i-do-as-a-private-investigator/

Overview of the industry

A breakdown of salary, employment rates and the general market
http://www.privateinvestigatoradvicehq.com/private-investigator-salary-how-much-can-you-expect-to-make-as-a-private-investigator/
https://www.bls.gov/oes/2018/may/oes339021.htm
https://neuvoo.ca/salary/?job=Private%20Investigator
https://www.indeed.co.uk/salaries/private-investigator-Salaries,-England

https://www.payscale.com/research/AU/Job=Private_Detective_or_Investigator/Salary
https://www.glassdoor.co.nz/Salaries/investigator-salary-SRCH_KO0,12.htm

Bureau of Labor Statistics
https://www.bls.gov/ooh/protective-service/private-detectives-and-investigators.htm

General how-to guides and blogs

An online magazine
http://pursuitmag.com/

An online magazine/network
https://www.pinow.com/

A list of resources for Australia
http://pitoolbox.com.au/

Advice and podcast for new investigators
http://www.privateinvestigatoradvicehq.com/

Marketing and business advice
https://investigatormarketing.com/resources/

Research resources and directory
https://www.einvestigator.com/

Research resources and directory for Australia
https://www.nettrace.com.au/

Online resources
http://www.private-investigator-info.org/

Electronic Frontier Foundation, online trends
https://www.eff.org/

Specific how-to articles

Refining web searches
https://support.google.com/websearch/answer/2466433

Report examples and templates
https://investigatormarketing.com/shop
http://pursuitmag.com/writing-the-perfect-investigative-report/

Some down to earth advice on how to become a P.I.
https://www.youtube.com/watch?v=ChHRHD_IDmM

Managing social media privacy
https://identity.utexas.edu/everyone/how-to-manage-your-social-media-privacy-settings
https://socialpilot.co/blog/ultimate-guide-manage-social-media-privacy-settings/

Social media marketing
https://investigatormarketing.com/social-media-private-investigators/
http://pursuitmag.com/social-media-marketing-for-pis/
https://www.linkedin.com/pulse/7-social-media-tips-private-investigators-chet-engstrom

Associations or support groups

National Association of Professional Process Servers
http://napps.org/

United States Association of Professional Investigators
http://www.usapi.org/

National Association of Investigative Specialists
http://www.pimall.com/nais/dir.menu.html

Links to P.I. associations by state
http://www.pimagazine.com/links/pi-associations-usa/

Links to international P.I. associations
http://www.pimagazine.com/links/pi-associations-international/

Association of Certified Fraud Examiners

http://www.acfe.com/

Worldwide Private Investigator Network
http://www.privateinvestigatornetwork.com/

Association of British Investigators
https://www.theabi.org.uk/
Institute of Professional Investigators
http://www.ipi.org.uk/

UK Professional Investigators Network
http://www.ukpin.com/

Training/certification institutions

American Board of Forensic Accounting
http://abfa.us/

Investigative Training, Florida
http://www.investigativetraining.org/

25 private Investigator training and education programs
https://www.pinow.com/articles/1115/top-25-private-investigator-training-education-2012

Licensing requirements

Overview of licensing requirements in Australia, UK, United States and Canada
https://en.wikipedia.org/wiki/Private_investigator#Across_the_world

Requirements in US states
https://www.einvestigator.com/how-to-become-a-licensed-private-investigator/

Links to licensing offices in the US
http://pursuitmag.com/resources/investigator-licensing/

Licensing authority in New Zealand
https://www.justice.govt.nz/tribunals/licences-certificates/pspla/

Equipment

You can also find a lot of items on Amazon
www.amazon.com

http://www.brickhousesecurity.com/
https://spyassociates.com/
http://spycity.com.au/
http://www.pimall.com
http://www.pigear.com/
https://www.lawmate.com.au/
https://www.eyetek.co.uk/
https://www.spysite.com/
http://www.detective-store.com/
https://gadgetsandgear.com/
https://www.spyequipmentuk.co.uk/
https://www.daytonaspyshop.com/
https://www.spygeargadgets.com/

Books and resources available on Amazon

Obviously, you're not just going to read one book. If you're anything like I was, you're going to read every book, article and online resource you can get your hands on. A book may contain exactly the same information as another book, but it says it in a different way that actually means something to you. So, it pays to be well read.

In fact, when I first started, I had read so many books and articles that it felt like I was already living the life of a P.I.!

I've reviewed several resources available on Amazon and rated them.

There is a lot of information out there, this should save you some time.

The Everything Private Investigation Book: Master the techniques of the pros to examine evidence, trace down people, and discover the truth - Sheila L. Stephens
http://amzn.to/2uXefL4

This book is definitely focused more on the tactics side of things, rather than becoming a private investigator. However, like other books in the 'Everything' series, it does offer a good overview of the industry and lifestyle of a P.I. It covers tactics, real stories and case studies.

This is also one book you'll probably find at your public library.

Usefulness (for becoming a P.I.): 3/5
Usefulness (for actual training): 3/5

Private Detective: Sleuthing: Become a P.I. - Gregory Emmerson
http://amzn.to/2w537vl
A very brief overview of a presentation Gregory Emmerson gave quite a few years ago. It covers in bullet point format: public records, surveillance, how to work with other agencies and undercover operations.

It is not useful as a guide on how to become a P.I.

Usefulness (for becoming a P.I.): 0/5
Usefulness (for actual training): 1/5

How to become a Private Investigator – David Ball (Editor: Dee Dee Young)
http://amzn.to/2uY6GUC

It says it's written as a course but is more a narrative format and is well laid out and researched. A little bit older now, but It's very easy to follow and goes into quite a bit of detail in the areas it covers (a little too much details in a lot of things that are outdated or you don't need to know). The first half covers how to become a P.I. and the second half covers how to do the actual work (with some good examples).

Usefulness (for becoming a P.I.): 4/5
Usefulness (for actual training): 4/5

The secrets to becoming a private investigator: A guide to private investigation as a career – Randy Bias
http://amzn.to/2hmabAN

More like a speech than a book, the lack of paragraphs and sections can be a little hard to follow. The writer clearly has plenty of experience in the field though and there are some good tips in here regarding getting your first job. He could have gone into more detail in a lot of areas, but it's a pretty good starting point that can lead to more research.

Usefulness (for becoming a P.I.): 3/5
Usefulness (for actual training): 3/5

The complete idiot's guide to private investigating, third edition – Steven Kerry Brown
http://amzn.to/2vh3wO7

As you'd expect from the 'idiot's guide' series, this contains a massive amount of information broken down into easy and actionable chapters. The first two sections contain information on how to get into the business, while the next three are related to actual training and techniques. I would recommend reading this one regardless of whatever else you read, as you're sure to find things in here that no other resource contains. It also has several useful links to online resources and databases.

Usefulness (for becoming a P.I.): 4/5
Usefulness (for actual training): 5/5

Private investigation: How to become a private investigator – Marcos Martinez
http://amzn.to/2uXONFp

A very brief overview of the different areas of private investigation, and common backgrounds of investigators. It doesn't go into any real detail and there are few actionable steps to take out of it.

Usefulness (for becoming a P.I.): 0/5
Usefulness (for actual training): 1/5

How to open & operate a financially successful private investigation business - Michael Cavallaro
http://amzn.to/2uXfQAB

A well-researched book on becoming a P.I., getting your license and starting your own business. It also covers being an intern at an investigative agency, something no other book does as well as this one. Definitely worth the read, it goes deep into a lot of areas.

Usefulness (for becoming a P.I.): 5/5
Usefulness (for actual training): 4/5

Private investigation 101 - Norma M. Tillman
http://amzn.to/3beCU6f

A light overview of a lot of areas of private investigation. It briefly touches on many points, however, contains a good overview of the different types of cases. It also contains an extensive list of ways to find information on and off-line. It's especially useful for tracing enquiries.

Usefulness (for becoming a P.I.): 3/5
Usefulness (for actual training): 5/5

END

Printed in Great Britain
by Amazon